SHEARSMAN
121 & 122

WINTER 2019 / 2020

EDITOR
TONY FRAZER

Shearsman magazine is published in the United Kingdom by
Shearsman Books Ltd
50 Westons Hill Drive
Emersons Green
BRISTOL   BS16 7DF

Registered office: 30-31 St James Place, Mangotsfield, Bristol BS16 9JB
(this address not for correspondence)

www. shearsman.com

ISBN 978-1-84861-678-3
ISSN 0260-8049

Subscriptions and single copies

Current subscriptions – covering two double-issues, each around 100 pages in length – cost £16 for delivery to U.K. addresses, £18 for the rest of Europe (including the Republic of Ireland), and £22 for the rest of the world. Longer subscriptions may be had for a pro-rata higher payment. Purchasers from North America will find that buying single copies from online retailers in the U.S.A. or Canada will be cheaper than subscribing. This is because airmail postage rates in the U.K. have risen rapidly, whereas copies of the magazine are printed in the U.S.A. to meet orders from online retailers there, and thus avoid the transatlantic mail.

Back issues from n° 63 onwards (uniform with this issue) cost £8.95 / $16 through retail outlets. Single copies can be ordered for £8.95 direct from the press, post-free within the U.K., through the Shearsman Books online store, or from bookshops. Issues of the previous pamphlet-style version of the magazine, from n° 1 to n° 62, may be had for £3 each, direct from the press, where copies are still available, but contact us for a quote for a full, or partial, run.

Submissions

Shearsman operates a submissions-window system, whereby submissions may only be made during the months of March and September, when selections are made for the October and April issues, respectively. Submissions may be sent by mail or email, but email attachments are only accepted in PDF form. We aim to respond within 3 months of the window's closure, i.e. all who submit *should* hear by the end of June or December, although for recent issues we have sometimes taken a little longer.

This issue has been set in Bembo with titling in Argumentum.
The flyleaf is set in Trend Sans.

Contents

Alexandra Sashe

Song of Autumn

We sow in the Land the cries
of the birds we don't follow –

we were chosen by Autumn to stay
and till with your eyes the sky.

We gather in barns
the sun and the shade
and leave in the dump air

imprints of our breath,
of our slow step,
as we wind the clocks of the field
with our faithful unflying hands.

The trees kneel and embrace the fog
and bury the roots deeper in sleep,
they were chosen by Autumn to give :
fruits for a fall, leaves for a wing.

We remain immobile among the days,
among the space of withered grass,
we learn from the trees to bury and yield,
to fly in sleep,
    to kneel and embrace.

And this bee and this grass fulfil their instant.

And I thirst and deny and travel

and make up for it
with a sign of the cross.

Instantwards, our hands
are dying premises. And the day is growing alive
as the hours are tolled.
Eyes winged with the weaving of nests upon the belfries
count our steps by quantities.

And the bells are full of air
and validation,
                    and

we breathe and deny and thirst.

When we lie on the grass, on the snow, on the sky
and tremble for hope, for light, for sleep,
with our naked harmless arms
nailed to the means
of our being

When we hear the voice of the silence, and wait
for our names to be called
to life,
        lengthened and spelt
among the clouds,
and our naked harmless hearts
be broken, cleansed and justified

When we see the imprints of our face
in the grass, in the snow, – and we search in the sky,
and abandon resemblance, harmony, knowledge,
and seek the harmless, the naked,
the eyes

When we wake up and partake of the green,
the white and the blue
layers of certainty, –

and release the hold and begin to be
        and begin to be

        And begin to be.

It is time to replace
the units of time
with the units of being without act,
with a tree growing down towards its shadow,
with the shadow describing its ultimate circle.

At the edge of the white blossoming field,
it is time to harvest the absence of hunger,
to develop transparent unfoldable wings,

to renounce to walk, and deny space, –
and collect its smallest
unbreakable fragments.

With the nascent melody of the silence,
with its intervals and the dying
echoes of steps and voices,
it is time –

to count the gold of denials,
to exit time
through its instant-long
            corridors.

via the candle's growing
down towards its purpose, via the snow
melting its stone-grown heart.
   via the wedded
wax and thaw water.

It is the last notes of the Song, carrying bread
to the mouth of fullness. It is our praise,
the embrace of our
frailty, love, duty. It is our
Song of the only recourse.

And the spring replaces us, stitch by stitch.
Our eyes are carried away beyond the sun.
In the puddles, the strangers search
for the reflections of our wings, –

it is our last Song,
once we have outlived the last.

Benjamin Balint

from Jerusalem Libraries

Library of the Custody of the Holy Land (Monastery of St. Savior)

An essay on pilgrimage and its benefits (*Del viaggio di Terra Santa*):
Jerusalem is a filigree work, with zoomorphic motifs, grotesques in black and light brown.

Jerusalem is a collection of medical recipes in Judeo-Arabic,
bearing an *ex libris* with the Virgin Mary,
belonging to one Mourkos (unidentified), whose family sold the volume after his death to the Library of the Custody for three Palestinian pounds.

Jerusalem is an antiphonary,
copied on vellum by different hands with pen-flourished decoration,
imperfect at the beginning and at the end,
and its colophon reads: "The copy was transcribed to perfection by…"

Jerusalem is a collection of interlinear comments about some important sentences of Christ, spoken before his crucifixion,
some titles and horizontal catchwords rubricated,
candle wax spotting the unbound leaves,
framed with floral festoon,
glossed in Latin on free endpapers from an earlier codex,
its edges mottled, the raised bands on the spine now loose.

Jerusalem delivered, in a precarious state of conservation owing to intensive use.

Schocken Library

Hear, O Israel, renew our days.
In the Dispersion, love the land where youth and blossoms bloom.

Footloose in Jerusalem, in the footsteps of Moses,
In the house of Herod, the faithful city, the gate of heaven, *La Cité de David*.

Love the fogs which ascend from the Dead Sea to the mountains of
Jerusalem, to the joy that is Jerusalem.
Love the intensity of the sun-rays measured on Mount Scopus.

Love the intensity of the ultra-violet rays in Palestine,
the haunted springs and water demons in Palestine (the upper
cretaceous and lower tertiary microfaunas),
the importance of dew in Palestine.

Scripta hierosolymitana: And the crooked shall be made straight,
And the script shall be made straight.

The three Scrolls of the Law that were found in the Temple court:
A Talmud written by the people in their own land, in secure and
recognized boundaries, emphatic words in biblical Hebrew, like
gems from the fountain.
A collective catalogue of Ingathering.
A handbook for proselytes.

Qumran Library (Dead Sea Scrolls)

A palimpsest of wisdom texts in an infrared ritual bath:
The copper scroll, the Temple Scroll, the Scroll of the War of the
Sons of Light Against the Sons of Darkness.

A letter sent from Ein Gedi concerning divine providence,
Or concerning a centurion, or concerning a concession of rights, or
concerning the balsam trade or the sale of a date crop.

The allegory of the vine,
Or a deed of pledge of a vineyard?

Minor prophets discovered in the Cave of Horror at Nahal Hever,
Or a list of false prophets?

Words of the luminaries, words to all the sons of dawn,
Or the lament by a leader?

Expositions on the patriarchs,
Or rebukes reported by the overseer?

A Hallelujah,
Or a writ of divorce?

The rule of blessings,
Or of curses?

Mysteries of messianic apocalypse,
Or a summons and counter-summons?

A meditation on creation, on the ways of righteousness,
Or mere scribal exercises?

*Note: These poems are wholly assembled from titles and catalog descriptions of
Jerusalem's historic libraries, raw material not intended to be have poetic resonan-
ces. Only the punctuation and prepositions have been altered.*

Lucy Hamilton

Meeting with the Elders

After Aw Tee Hong's sculpture: 'The River Merchants'

Singapore & Borneo are steeped in childhood mystery
the myth of my mother & the bishop we called Father

his stories of canoes & longhouse | tales of voodoo
and the pulsing beauty of rainforest | river & delta

I sensed my father's resentment | his fear I'd be bewitched
and work for the bishop entranced by fables & magic

But other schools drew me to the music of the East End
& Brixton with their vibrant rhythm of languages

& patois | dialects & slang | Today printing photographs
I took last May of Singapore street art & sculpture

as J explored his old work haunts & office buildings
now dwarfed by skyscrapers | I place the pavement art

of multinational faces as a backdrop for the bronze
Scottish merchant | Chinese trader | Malay chief

who could be a group of scholars or philosophers
exchanging myths with the Indian & Chinese migrants

loading goods into a bullock cart | and import an early
work photo of J to this meeting with the Elders

Box Brownie & Cameo

I print the photo of the bishop and my mother
sitting together on the grass at the house

that was snapped on Grandad's old Box Brownie
all those years ago| then cut out the two figures

and jiggle them between text balloons
to create a point of balance| These egg-shaped

balloons hold air-mail script from Malaysia
which speaks of *the growing tension & uneasiness*

among the young especially amongst the Chinese
but I'm transfixed by the brooch on my mother's

hand-knitted jumper| the shell cameo I'd stroke
as a toddler running my fingers over the relief

The second slightly smaller blue balloon sits
at a diagonal to the first |linking quotations

The Americans have proved overwhelmingly
that an outside force is a waste of lives & time

bridged by the photo bringing my mother closer
I hope you have more news of the children

And although the cameo's detail is out of focus
I still know it doesn't depict Nyx the winged

Goddess of the Night carrying her two children
Just as I'm sure the bishop's unease *I do feel concerned*

about their welfare doesn't refer to the boy twins Hypnos
the God of Sleep and Thanatos the God of Death

I can't see the cameo distinctly but remember
that the upper shell's white & the lower's red-brown

The contrast & translucence of the tiers resonate
with the bishop's distant writing *because of such close*

association with them all in the past and my mother's
French-tinged speaking voice| her body warmth

& aura when I was four needling her again & again
to tell me the story of the three white agate figures

depicting a large winged angel carrying two babies
Now his words *& because they are your children* conjure

my mother repeating the myth of the angel's arrival
bringing her the twin-gift of my sister and me

Gerrie Fellows

An Inventory of Natural Dyes

            A herb
            brittle now
            a spike of buds
Weld   the dyers' weed

            the only metals
            mordants to set the colour
            tin   unripens to lemon
                        sharp on the taste buds
                        at the back of the tongue

            melded to the felt of wool
            sweet mulled yellow
            of mignonette

                        my mother's hand keeping this
                        bright coin.

Marigold   with *alum*
            verges from lemon to grey
                        might be a new colour
                        in the corner of her eye

                        an alchemist
                        panning for the pure gold
                        substance of the world.

Alkanet   summer's net of blue
             makes red, they say
             grows like a weed
             gives up its root
             woody fibres   pale core

                     Is this our blue familiar
                     makes strange
                     dark   foreboding
                     purples?

Brazilwood   a dazzling stranger
               deep red at evening

               in the small light of day
               vanishes
                       a puzzled shade
                       not fast to sunlight.

Logwood   samples from chips
             soaked 4 hrs
             boiled until almost black

                     By what name
                     shall we call colour
                     that cannot be   without light?

If I knew nothing
of ribboned bark
Eucalyptus bleached in heat
a light that takes colour

would I say ice of this lemon green
would I say spring might come?

Poplar buds top-dyed with *madder*
a darkening
as of weather
in a temperate zone

north light's
long shadows.

After winter
Fustic a bright must
pales to the horizon
or deepens to a field edge
to snow grass
and bleached tussocks.

After winter:
an inventory of colour

Onion skin   a papery bloom of
                 honey or sunlight
                            the balm of matter

                 she might once have called to us
                 to witness.

Indigo   taken yellow from the vat
                 shaken to blue
                 in the element of our breath
                 curious insoluble

                            What shall we call
                            that colour
                            not of water but air

                            refracted light
                            of
                            our shared molecules?

Kate Schmitt

Stahlhelm

Mesniac, August 29, 1917
In memory of my grandfather, Mario Perera

Like Autolycus, I inherited
Hermes' ability to steal without being caught.
No one's to blame for whatever
it was – a wrong turn, over the top
alliances – the mise-en-scène is co-created.
A mountain regimenteer is outmoded,
wearing a helmet that can't shield him.

I was charging the machine-gun nest,
my bayonet points pointing toward the hill
when Apollo, in an updraft, caught
my oak-bark hat into his capacious till,
making of me a bare-headed little light
brigade. *Here's a fair exchange*
for the soothsayer's art, he said,
and I'm keen on Italian workmanship.

Without a glance back to a dead German,
who made a kind of gift,
I made a kind of graft.
I made a pledge to often glance back
to the double graft with bullet-deflecting

shrapnel, to a scaly pinecone-stamped
doubloon that shifted
into my skull, postponing
knowledge of what they say
is always the same message.

In Sintra

Present-day royals like the Kennedys can play at stealth-
leaping, like polar bears on a shrinking ice floe,
but the flask that restores balance, grace and youth,
is there for the taking, for any who visit Portugal's no-
eat, no-drink zone. A flow

of frigid air from the sculpted greenery
nips. An otherworldly glow entrances
even as our crew pulls off an extraordinary exit.
The venerable sculptor had brushed aside wet greenery,
king-sized, overgrown potted plants in courtyards,

that only half-hid black granite and rose quartz
busts of royalty, portraits of kings
who were overthrown like potted plants
from the rotting courts of Europe.
Chips had flown. Sitters had schmoozed

under royal palms and busted-up black granite.
Socialism had drawn its hypotenuse
across Europe. Schmooze
had given way to schlep. South America
will never cede to socialism, they said. Draw an hypotenuse,

do the math. I'd thumbed through my Baedeker
before schlepping here from North America,
flying out of Kennedy. I'd returned by stealth
into this myth not exactly thumb-nailed in Baedeker,
in hopes of drinking from Persephone's flask.

In the Dark

A man who had left the groves
of academe, and now plays acoustic,

was floundering in Burlington, batting zero,
getting stoned. A distraught Yuri Zhivago type

who could never stay put, he figures
he'll move to Iceland, foot the bill

by performing at house parties.
One gig played completely in the dark

returns him to the laws that govern
nature. Someone brings him a coke, and

the lilac lady's rhythms fire a flash, grounding
him like a buried rainbow,

prompting him to realize
that all the patrons are

blind. He settles into
his groove,

steps onto his own
fugitive interfluve.

Rachael Clyne

Plague Times

At Passover, a finger is dipped into our cup of wine and a drop splashed, as each plague is named. We do not rejoice.

I   ***Blood***   דָּם

On hands, in every breath in belly of whale, in gullet and gizzard, from every littered shore, we turn the seas incarnadine.

II   ***Frogs***   צְפַרְדֵּעַ

After ice-melt, I pull three frogs, bloated and stinking, from the pond. Can we afford to lose them? Slugs will flourish in this unlikely spring.

III   ***Flies***   כְּנִים

Feast on our flesh, wriggle their fatted way, before winging off to island havens, offshore nests, to leave a humanless world.

IV   ***Wild Beasts***   עָרוֹב

In Chernobyl, wolf-law rules empty dachas, factories. Bears refill forests. Here, Adonis Blue butter-flies will thrive on Salisbury Plain. Rats and dogs will shelter in car shells.

V   ***Cattle plague***   דֶּבֶר

Play-barns that have swings and muzak, are no place for chickens. Carousel feed-troughs rotate past cattle. Pigs gaze through gratings at a crack of sky.

VI   ***Boils***   שְׁחִין

This winter virus has no end. The people cough their way into summer. Vaccinations, rumoured to be toxic, do not help. An unreliable source blames chem-trails.

VII   *Hail*   בָּרָד

First, snow, so deep. That night, rain. By morning the window – solid ice. On the ground, black ice, invisible. We could not step outside. Next day, hail thuds onto the roof. Hail, snow and the sound like corpses falling – these are surely plague times.

VIII   *Locusts*   אַרְבֶּה

Gobbling hoards turn Friday black, as they swarm through shopping malls, stampede for their white gods. Trample one other for plasma screens.

IX   *Darkness*   חֹשֶׁךְ

A firmament of LED glare and twinkle of red and white lights thread highways through the undarkened night. The only visible stars are on the ground.

X   *Death of Firstborn*   בְּכוֹרוֹת מַכַּת

Floods destroy the power station. Fish without scales, tumour-ridden. Cover the ocean to its farthest coast. There will be no offspring.

XI   *Parting of Waves*

Red the ocean, gone the ice, gone coastline. No more trips to the sea-side. No sandcastles. No bargains to buy. No people to eat up everything No trees. No creatures to catch. No insects to bite. No birds to shoot
No   property
to   buy   No   planes
     to   fly   No   fish
       to   fry   No   God
        to   part   the

     waves
              just
    burning
          bushes

Chris Emery

Dear Delys

Good morning, Delys, this life again
explains its density in roof slates.
No one pervades the middle distance.
Your days are peppered with children.
Do not adhere to gloom.
Delys, meanwhile, parades infesting
ungovernable republics, modern ceremonies
fail to invest that ginger magic
necessary for the General to exhibit
guitar practice.
Somewhere, Delys, fabrics sit in a welter
of colour on an earth floor with
severed legs seeping. No one should know
how memories end. Let's end and
listen to Byrd's *Nunc Dimittis*
and recall this local perfection, Delys,
so soon after our return,
everyone happy with the right measure
of blame and someone to blame
for permanent twilight.
Delys, no one's arms have yet been torn.
In the middle distance, long lines
toot and moan, toot and moan
past grey tired buildings in the rain.
The slates tip our fears into years.

How to Be a Poet

In the cold window slurred
with condensation, beakers
of dark rain—your childhood stopped
in glass and teak shadows
leaving their regular art
beside angled reflections, maimed
and mute, calmly looking at
the blind garden, so banal
and scary in this stress dream,
we want the tight words out,
all the birds scurry, flightless,
picking grit in some black snow.
Unless a new memory
of the simple city leaves
a photograph one evening,
weighing despair, each childless
and ineffectual mood
pressed for time in that sad bar
and the wind's cold coils picking
through our warm street where we lurch
towards a frightening door
and then step through into this:
cold and rancid, chattering,
groping through lit motes, half mad.
Exiled in the lightless room
find the voice inside the voice—
no precision or belief,
secular hours filled with sleet
and everything wasted, you're
kissing moth delivered news
and learning the body is
its own amanuensis,
curled on the ruins, fastened
to each meagre line, each step
revealing more abstract years,
sheltering in some lost name.

Advice to Young Writers

1. You will meet your teeth at the Walsall school show.
2. Your everyday pants will never pass security at a midday Mecca.
3. Announce all secrets with your Top of the Town spider dance.
4. Naturally, life will be cash negative on most verse points.
5. Remember bath hair cannot be redeemed as the days pour out.
6. Never kill for the mung bean stew.
8. Know every soiled moon will get worse.
9. Prepare each towelling robe for the blue afternoon.
10. Do not write about the gas works.

James Turner

Onset

It comes
and grows and stays. It's awful.
General Practitioner. Crisis Team. Hospital.
Nurses. Psychiatrist. Medication. Side-effects.
Panic. Shouting. Crawling on the floor.
Delusional fears more real than truth. You find
you have to relearn, one by one, every routine
of living, how to walk normally, talk normally,
hold a cup, and later, how to go shopping.
Nothing comes naturally any more. Your smile
is like a simile. Don't expect instant recovery,
they keep on telling you. Instant recovery!
What the *hell* is it about you that makes them
think you might expect *that*? Minimalism,
in life as in music, isn't brevity,
it's repetition. "You cannot step into
the same river twice." Not so, Heraclitus!
It never used to be, but now it's always
the same bloody river. "One day is like another."
That's more like it, Heraclitus! And yet
there is a flow, as imperceptibly slow
as creeping glass, a centuries-old window-pane
found to be thicker at the bottom. You call it
recovery to keep friends happy but you still need
strong coffee to counter the depressing effect
of antidepressant pills. Evenings are best.
Knowing each dosed-up day will be rounded
with dosed-up sleep, you can feel safe,
as if in a comfortable cul-de-sac
protected from the future by a wall
as soft as death itself.
As if.

For a Start

For a start there's no poetry in it.
Poetry, apart from being words,
is that non-verbal admixture
without which depression
rules the realm of consciousness.
Depression is when you reach the end of the line.
Depression isn't sadness, isn't an emotion at all
but a blockage, a block in which emotion
is frozen, though fear flows readily under it,
and around it float wisps
of general negativity
the theory of whose erratic movements
still awaits its Albert Einstein.
Even guilt, at not being able
to feel emotions such as love and gratitude,
is stuck there, frozen
almost.

Words cannot convey depression, but with *The Idiot,*
Crime and Punishment, The Brothers Karamazov
and *The Devils*, Dostoyevsky get close.
Think of it: depression so severe that reading
and re-reading those four great Russian novels
not only keeps you going, but actually cheers you up.
The weird light they shed throws into relief
a wealth of detail embroidered on the black bedspread.
The importance of suffering, the mechanics of cruelty.
the temptation of suicide: Dostoyevsky
knows, like no other author, the basement room
where light so seldom penetrates. His books
are the only books I can bear to read. Empathy
isn't the same as imagining *yourself*
in another's place, as you will know if you've
been clinically depressed and people have tried
to empathise.

Annemarie Austin

Razzle-Dazzle

Yip Harburg: 'Stars in the night
                Blazing their light
                Can't hold a candle -
                To your razzle-dazzle.'

It was Mary Zekiel explained
how an angel had parked its wings
there on the coat-and-hat stand
just inside the front door in the dim.
She was presumed to know about such things.

But I always thought of you not-quite-dressed, anyway,
taking out the pins.

                (Queen Elizabeth's costumes
were built of independent segments from
separate chests - undersleeves, oversleeves,
three-part skirts and bodice fronts - anchored
for the moment by bright pins that clicked
and pinged to the floors as she went away.)

…when they stood, they let down their wings.

If any of us tried to fly by sewing
pillows to armholes and making
makeshift wings, they'd be in trouble,
Mary Zekiel reminded. Such things
were always professional undertakings.

But I thought of you sloughing off your sleeves, anyway,
undoing fastenings.

                    (On Queen Elizabeth's
dresses jewels were transferred from bodice
to bodice as required, knots of pearls unknotted
to star in those portraits sent to the ends of
the kingdom in her stead, to embody her self –
so suffer embedding in poison or stabbing with
hog bristles, burning. Men died for such acts.)

And he put forth the form of an hand, and took me by a lock of mine head.

Oh look at you without your wings. What a
pretty thing.
                    What a smooth and luminous figure
at the end of the passage going away.
                                        Today
Mary Zekiel didn't need to make me aware of
your arrival.
                    For you flared and dazzled where
the shadows should have been deepest.
                                        There are
dark shapes of you left behind in my eyes.

Nail File

Think of filing down the Atlantic Ocean
which widens every year
at roughly the rate of
a fingernail growing.

There was a rock in that ocean.
There was a bobbing raft.

He stood on the rock and saw
nothing in the water. Nothing
should use that raft
to reach his rock.

So he hauled in the raft by its rope
and tied it to the rock.

After a while he was sure he saw
how this rock diminished as
the Atlantic widened.

And so stood on one leg to be
smaller and more narrow.

He certainly saw how raft and rope
were frayed by the fret of
rock against water.

That was when he thought of
filing down the ocean.

Alison Brackenbury

Census Returns

Lower Snowden 1851
Reservoir Cottage 1881
Cramp Pool Lane 1891

    for my family

No. They leave nothing I can find,
stout baskets, mud-drenched petticoats,
although their sorrows shaped my mind,
those housemaids, master wheelwrights,
tan oak leaves, tough on Shropshire wind,
tunes trapped in throats.

Homes for the poor were swept away.
Wild south wind rushes Cramp Pool Lane
where my grandfather blinked to day.
Where their gates swung, new hedge shines thin.
Oaks, then slender, rule my sky.
Hard acorns rain.

My young great-grandmother made homes
with John, her restless gamekeeper,
one, a brick cottage pines clasp close
by sunlit miles of reservoir.
To their plain gate a gun dog strolls,
black Labrador.

Why do we move? Here he shaped all,
oak, ash and elm, her father George,
in one wheel for the heedless Hall.
Let sons ride rails to London's roar.
Hannah and he made ten grow tall
beside this forge.

How my small grandfather loved birds!
Buzzards his father's levelled gun
tumbled from sky, can now scale cloud.
On the long hillside, high past pain
while tractors plough, how they cry, loud
down Cramp Pool Lane.

The river in the city: the Witham

Then as I bumped my suitcase back
along the Brayford wall
I saw the slender crested grebe
land on her morning pool.
Quick as a lover's blink, she dived
three times. Clear as a call,
wide, rippled rings, white watchful sky,
and nothing caught at all.

Come in

The house is tall. The house is warm.
And through a door, past books and flowers,
I glimpse the old man, tiny now
in his deep chair, sunk in deep hours.
And through it all a woman flits,
bright, anxious still, as when we kept
houses where babies cried, then slept.

Adam Flint

Banish & Protect

"It's hedgerows." —Jhonn Balance

Gentle commands play golden and balanced
light along modest children's arms

where down
                    spun or
        in full sun flickers

and hastens the fasting shadows observe

★

                    cult-sick
now as when heanling
laid by forced ferment
at the leaper-gapped
hedgerows lank and drear
in forb of balsam
bristly cleaver
severing the venerated
                    head
for safety

★

                    a ritual impulse
                    repetitive effect

to come to to the understory
traipse again the mayweed waysides
for all their ragged worth

in the way hedges and thickets
speak to the need for secrets

in the way the darkness
           babbles under the earth

            to seep light flower

            to see plight flower

dark birdsong dawn

★

winged calls that seed the day

the internal mell of welcomes outstayed
assembles itself and sings

as light behind a lenten moon
warms the cones to open

            green leaves brighter than blood
            red dew point petals

★

            the parched lurch
            for the dew leaves

a film on the cell-petalled visage

                  colonising
lorn ditch-sides

little white-lair morning life

blooms as lunar
human-spurner

    deigning further to wake

*

    hover-flies and
    fox-coloured commas
    bask on posts
    the divine adorn

    a dawn trace
    of their visitation
    under twig-clog
    gnarl of haw

    and alder
    fallen walnut shells
    tipped from squirrel's dreys

embedded in earth where snails have left
their crispened caves to cloud

*

    in the way the tangential thrives
direction dwindles and appals
rigorous wakings ignited midstride
    chin to the chest to the headwind
down and out the arms for balance
into a listing sun

                    yielding like water
                              exhaustingly so
            undulant light capsizing
torment till blooms slipped and leaved
cede to towering umbels

                the night breeze sways
                the stalked parsley
                stars oxen favour

*

votive libations sealed in tin
hidden under thickets
for the god to mislay
undergo devotional recovery
the draught as soon as raised

to honour the degraded
divinity in open field
the rends lit risenward fray

                sadness done with
                venery and wild things

                sunset brideless
                less red lord

the least glimmer
wept and fought for

            reverses
            merkstaves

*

young charge without might and flutter
in games with the sun

meadow-grass lit by rounding figures
ancients moved in spaces

in the way I become of no
sound and those

     spaces

         in the way

★

the spent are left under hedgerow

a course bluffed across the endless meads for main roads
as lant skips
         astride a stile
     and scans the golden dale

deletion of fields
     of field
     of cloth
     of gold

         by a glinting wind

Andrew Duncan

SCALE OF CHAINS

Proposal for a Monument to the Empire

Lord Justice Nuremberg
Under the sign of the picked skull
Holding out the findings on the dissenters and injured, contends
this.
It was all worthwhile.
A star led us at the pace of a cannon-shot.
Entire landscapes were devastated,
Labour shackled to the timbers, below deck, was made mobile
And brought to where the work is.
A hundred battles with paths cleared through the ranks,
A score of famines, tightness in the market –
All this was part of the wide straight track.
A kinetic global future ordered our paces.
He has chicken eyes and goes on crow's claws.

The keelless Monitor class with gun platform
Moves up-river to stand-in close to villages.
Throw of shot, flaring thatches.
Flexible power to delete what hears it
Opening up the back country. Unsealing the trade.
So many states overthrown that would set constraints,
So much territory made as passable as the air.
Free trade zone. Clear land title. Pacified tribes.

Before we open the record of costs
Or even give the file a name
We could state what was putatively abridged, the rights.
What was the title of a person,
Being Irish or Senegambian, to their life?
How what has not yet had reprisal
Could be found as a good,

"

Whose utter loss has a price?
Was this department of State quite reckless?
We thought settling ownership was the whole song.
What do the numbers say?
Who ever collected them,
Who kept an account of the lost?
What testimony is offered by those who are not living?

The assembly of property owners will have their commodity,
Endure together and enjoy in severalty.
Ratio dicendi written on human parchment,
Stipulations cut on soft blemishing flesh.
The justice of the slaughterhouse finds
No mistakes were made,
Clinching his conclusion
Before joining hands in a hymn.

Geography

Eyes. Scales. Feathers.
Oak hull, pine barrels for the catch,
Lying on the banks, one day out from Yarmouth.
As the herring leave the sea in their vessels of twine
The gulls leave the sky in their net of feathers.
As the one flock expels a scream
The other is learning to breathe.

On the deck, shuffling in herring eyes
The poet stoops at the knee, who said
He throned her in the gateways of the world.
The LORD set Britain to spearhead the out-thrust of Europe
Land regiments and cannon on every separate shore
Vacate the authority of a hundred kings
And chain the shores together as empire.
Thus the LORD
Working His geological CAD software
Moves Britain up from some bank near Canada

To set it down hard by Flanders.
The North Sea – was in the right place.
The mouth of the Baltic had to be constricted, near-blockade.
He was pleading for his baronetcy. *It must be here somewhere.*
Damn your theology. Execrations on your doctrine and its doctors.
Scour from the sky this deity.

By the dock, the gulls abound on the feasts of fish–guts
Careless on excess perceived as wealth.
A pipe adjusted to discharge into their mouths.
Natural peak values and natural decline.

A Statue Park

Mesopotamia, in 1930 designated as
A refuelling stop for air passage to India.
Held down by air power
Experimentally. Unrest in the villages, good visibility.

Projecting power without touching the ground.
A statue park recording the effects of blast
An optic nerve shattered.
Wax simulates the grain of bone sheared
When a bomb fragment tore through his thigh.
Esoteric the effects on tissue.
The cortex registered the wave form, as an ear does
Tender to each moment of energy.

The separated parts of the curved bomb casing
Elements that get carried away of buildings, it might be bricks,
–as transmitted impact.
The great clap of air itself, as blast
Acts in the medium of flesh.

What did he say, before the descent completed?
Did he know what an aerial bomb was?
Did he know this was a visit from the ruler?

The hole that shrapnel tore in his head
Recorded in polychrome wax. True to life.

Between St James' Park and Chatham House
Hundreds of figures in knots,
Standing on the steps or seated at tables.
Blue–black tinge of the skin.
Should these too be forgotten?
Reflexive thought dedicated to your death
Refraction when a sound wave enters a new medium.
Declining a new catalogue of anatomy.

The projection of malice without looking in someone's face.
Claws of air without the keratin
Grip without a bird
Cut the skin without leaving a mark
And stop the brain.

Project for a Monument

There is trouble counting them.
A town full of rooms which would be filled with nothing except
people counting the dead. The records show the flow of money but
not the tariff of the dead.
Set clerks to write a biography of all the people who died because an
empire was being built with them as a foundation. A pebble for each
dead human. Build a beach of pebbles.
Build a street of banks. In each bank a floor of tellers. Set them to
count all the gold brought in by the commerce of an empire. Set
them to write the biography of that gold – how it was both abstract
and substance, detaining the beauty of the air to adorn the rich. Build
a beach of gold.

The project allows for a plot at what is now Chatham House Terrace,
The Mall, and St James' Park to be sealed off with a precinct and
become the permanent installation site for the ship *Threadneedle*. It

is a replica of a slave-ship whose keel was laid in Liverpool in the 1780s, realised in granite from Cromarty. The deck is cut away to allow the visitor to see down into the business end of the affair: the slave deck, with 120 solidly built stanchions, robust enough to hold the cargo in their proper stations. Massive beams resist and steady that dissident strain. Disposed around the vessel are statues of slaves in glass enamel with inlays of gemstones displaying realistically in several colours the special marks of whiplashes and chafing sores around the fetter touches. Others hold their mouths open to show, in varieties of tropical wood, the effect of scurvy on their gums. Some of the existing statues of heroes of the Empire on Chatham House Steps are to be retained *in situ*, found objects as part of the monumental ensemble. The sails are made of flint precision-ground to the requisite fineness. The cables are made of whalebone, ingeniously whittled. The pink and carmine-tinged granites and intarsias are a conscious citation of the City office blocks of the years after Big Bang. Around the ship a sea is realised in sand and reflective foil, a reference to the precinct around the earliest Egyptian temples with their mounds rising above the primordial sea, in the moment of emergence of dry land, an acknowledgment of African roots. They are the limitless dank waters of the inert god Nun. Its edge is marked by a wall with elaborate niching, the 'temple façade', in calcite rendered to imitate reed matting. The creative scheme was designed by members of the New Triumphalist group, with a stress on the neglected values of expensive materials and grandiose scale.

Permanent security and surveillance cameras will be needed at the perimeter of the site.

Corporate funding has been pledged on the understanding that the new park will please all political factions, recording fine craftsmanship and keen commercial sensibility as well as the inevitable collateral damage.

The path is being sponsored by a famous marine insurance firm. Staffordshire china figurines showing the shareholders in the vessel are also on sale. They wear stove-pipe hats and have mutton-chop whiskers.

To lay a beach to which a sea of salt would bring a ship of stone.
A stone ship that sinks through the earth
And sails in search of water.

Monument to 60 Irish Phonemes

Stones standing for lost sounds
sounds carrying lost sense on soft air

a row of matches and differences
all learnt by a mouth

rhymes by classes
as the phoneme inventory is so large –
a sound couldn't find its like
so p goes with b

the gap between single and double narrow r
seized in flight by a native ear
and broken by imitation

thousands of names
the corrected learning
of those whose names hunger remembered

the disposal of sound in tiny steps
stretching out to an evening of recital

wind blowing through a thorn-bush, *an sceach*
torn into a cluster of separate sounds

disposal of syllables in a ring –
the last closing with the first, *dunadh*

the knowledge piled up and kept at Louvain or Douai
books without dispersal or flaw
of men without children
sound without incarnation

why they always say take a song
as if it were rushing by and they caught it

words breaking down
slur sl sep syll sios scrios

Habitat Destruction

A watercolour is lifelike in tints of plumage
The bird was once lifelike
Where fields and pastures
Are now swallowing every goodness.
This bird's young did not prosper,
Their young never fledged.
The painting is delicate and soundless.

Where was a fair and blooming land
Held without papers by a sort of kindred memory
Giving sustenance to hundreds with no export
The region is now property in the King's eye
Yielding so much per year in specie
Ditches clean and woods lightened
Cleared of whatever bred and wandered here.

There lacked nothing for the land to become endowed estates
But that the population sicken and die.
The turning of the territory into wealth
Was the razing of everything that moved,
The devastation of whatever it reared and which enjoyed it.

Nameless sound bounced off still water perhaps.
The clay beneath the land you see
Measured with cords and split by fences,
An ossified horizon dwindling by the year,
Is the people who once lived here.
Their voices said what was not convenient.
Some of their halls now used for cattle –
Marks of fabrication without saws still in sight.
Stray sounds catching at not quite meaning.

Colonies of Self-esteem

Scheme of concord covering 36 rooms
In elegant repetition
Training expectations
To miss whatever diverges.
A significant collection
Made pure by distortion;
Marble eye that sees only one colour.
Bequeath libraries replete with this.

Feathers like darts flurry off the glinting coat,
Lift the body into the sky
Flaws scale away like melting flakes
Ego as hero reared on magnificent thews
Pink with affluence of blood
Towering and tapered
In an arch over the world.
The depletion of resistance
To extend a false perfection
A globe dissolving into wealth.

Possession stretching deep into the past
Extending into the visible sky
And by entails binding the wishes of the future.
Knowledge as fixed enclosures
Grasping in each direction
To conceal dissent and decay
To record frozen wishes.

Reforming the map the way they grasp a coin,
Blurring its lines through water.
Webs of loss and damage
Retouched into adorning motifs.
Remodelling the imperfect asset.
The reproduction in detached terms of egoism without bounds.
In Latin parchments

Clauses asserting land rights
Are worked out like theology.

Change the laws to complete dominion,
Train history to a set of analogies.
It's a globe because all its radii are perfect,
Their slants wrenched straight.

A landscape remodelled for rapid transit,
A map like skin corrected to beauty.
Remap the minds of others
Their tenuous rights. Their birds' contracts.
Animating creatures to act as staff on the estates
Through a process of de-animation
Starting in childhood.
Our security
Is the curtailment of their wishes.
Their identification with what subdues them
Is the fruit of fine scholarship.

Errors on the microscopic scale
Located by new lenses; light straightened by better glass,
Pursuing concord to the utmost ends of perception,
Grasping whatever existed
And macerating it fine
And crushing it into the filling of symmetry as pigment,
Losing its wishes, its language, its idioms; its own likeness
Strained to symmetry to the last limb of a classic figure.
A picture repainted at the end of each day

Other cultures have laws.
If this is what it is
Knowledge of something else
Is inexact.
Rights to air do not
Lend themselves to proof.

The Dumb Book

An leabhar balbh, the dumb book,
Said by someone who possessed it then
To have been written by Seamas Mac Fhir Bhisigh
Maybe around 1560.
This book is lost.

Maybe the book of lost things,
The Book Dumb while other books speak
How could it be a book with no voice?
A collection of things that can't be said
A *leabhar* of things that can't be said any more.

Maybe a list of things that had no voice
Of things that would never speak again
Of things that could be known but not said
Of people whose voices did not carry far.

Of things that could not be remembered after time away.

Leabhar balbh
Of undocumented inherited rights
Of families that ceased to exist
And lands that disappeared from under them
Due to improvements to the law.

Seamas, from a family of scribes and genealogists,
In Sligo.
Firbissius, Firbissy. Forbès.

Repository

Display the feather
Of a bird that no longer nests or flies.
A feather cannot signal regret.
Its bright eye displays the status of a bird,
It has no off position.
The status is now down, and carcass.
For us regret is indigenous.

The judge finds
There is a deficit in the budget for truth.
If there is no tribunal which will protect these rights
The rights have no substance.
It is a vapour.
Pool of colour in a repository
That no-one visits.
The republic of mites, eaters of keratin,
Strip regalia of dead raptors.

From display to taxonomy. From flight to store-room.
The toxins of preservation leaching, discolouring.
A colony of things that live on flakes of skin
Spreading progeny in the hall of stuffed specimens.
Lords of the wealth of pelts.
A natural abundance that can only decline.
Exotic but factual.
This is mite heaven and they attribute it to their laws.

Rushika Wick

Through the Eyes of the Plastic Madonna

Driver:

Got to slam the brakes hard now, coast left,
give him a safe berth – how far depends on
how far gone the eyes read, and
you can't say exactly… it's not a science.

Those who feel invisible,
spirits as sensitive as trembling air above sea,
will recoil in a millisecond if the temperature
shifts slightly,

but beware the New Emperors,
heart-in-throat dangerous,
dressed with ice-precision they
spike spleens on holiday – don't give a shit.

Road Walker:

Nothing to lose by wading out,
hopes will swim around me as they always do,
don't take much notice of me.
My birth sign is Cancer, children
recoil when they hear that,
I'm amongst the bulrushes
blowing in the wind,
waiting for a hot breeze to lift
so I can flower,
become a feather for a season.

Plastic Madonna on the Dashboard:

And here it is, this intimate moment;
subject/ object
fate/ choice
where these two strangers are pre-collided,
compressed into the very stuff of life and
sending consciousness ahead,

everything is signal and reading,
time blooms a bright passage
and they become animal again –
hyper-alert with wings crushed
against the 33 bones of their spines

(a split second error in call or response
will dice reality)

and somehow it's always a dance
with the odds stacked,
a gold-blown cheat from the skies.

Jeri Onitskansky

Spring Fever

…and last night my bed
was surprised!
My bed had never seen

anything like it!
Marital bed
of the snore and the fart

upon which me
and my lover
swam each other's blissfully

flooded *palazzi* –
Ex-husband's pyjamas
thankfully dead in a drawer

like a flattened opossum.
Beyond the skylights,
cumulus tongued the delicate tips

of each still-naked
tree as if to cause giggling
all round as when

Dr E asked a patient
what he found funny. He said,
well, my situation

is pretty funny.
She said, what's so
funny about your situation?

He said,
well, being out of control
is kind of funny.

Praying While Marilyn Sleeps

…Co-star Marilyn Monroe was absent from the festivities…
Brownsville Herald, November 11, 1958

Dearest God

who are possibly as helpless as suds
swept out of church doorways

or in arrogance maybe you strut
across these roofs like a peacock –

topping and tailing, I lie staring
at Marilyn's toes painted the colour

of her kisses. As you can hear,
her snores are the snores of a man.

Marilyn dreamt of buckets
laden with stars. We found

starlight in the dregs and you
made it come up ravenous.

We love you for this, O Song
in the fan we sweat to each long night.

(from *Time Travel*)

Marilyn Exits the Cold War

The lie and its recipient,
in some shady but ultimately
legitimate negotiations,
agree upon a reality whereby
in lieu of a general congruence
between the recipient's
memory of events
and what actually happened,
there arises in time when
the lie is exposed, an emptiness
that is actually Marilyn
gone elsewhere, her amber hair
flying backwards.

(from *Time Travel*)

Clark Allison

Commonality

the topicality of inadvertence
leaving few traces
in the transit from
Mercury to the underworld
not unlike purgatory
there might be no getting out
reasoning or intuition
excitability quelled by ill feeling
there may have been a common denominator
but it pared
far too much away
every bag you bring back
is just mostly flotsam and dross
material gathers
seen a many good things
though not recently
until the rain when it came
turned everything to mud
to nitrogen cycle fodder
frenetic change
followed by a protracted and baffling middle
don't know if it's got or needs
five years or fifty

The Walk Home

while earlier it was
come as you are
it's not Sunday
and the specialness of occasion
needs no fanfare
but being hyper critical
one is apt to note
something out of place
getting the message
and even just what was missed
as one walked home alone
particular attention to beginnings
and endings, relieved or
gratified or sorry
and who's going back
or even why
if the credit's good

Paul Rossiter

Islanded

dark blue, whitecapped
waves fill the lower half of the window

heathery hills the upper half, and then

as the boat rolls, the window
frames only sky

*

approaching the island

a hundred yards offshore
the smell of cow shit on the wind

*

a curve of beach
a jetty
a low rounded hill
leaning gravestones and a roofless chapel

    await the thick deft BB pencil
    of Wilhelmina Barns–Graham

*

horizontal bands of colour
reach to a low horizon:

a drystone wall spotted with yellow lichen
a brilliant strip of grass

a fire-red straggle of wind-blown montbretia
slick black rain-wet tarmac
          richly smirched by the recent passage
          of a trotting herd of beeves
ribbons of yellow and brown seaweed
ruffled water tinged turquoise by the sandy seabed
          darkening further out to deeper then deeper blues

on the opposite shore
banks of mottled brown seaweed slope up to
red-roofed houses and a gently curved horizon
where two wind-turbines stand tall against grey sky

          small boats heave at their anchors
                    in an insistent westerly wind
          seabirds bob among whitecaps

          cloud shadows and sunshine
          constant changes of light

low grey clouds head rapidly eastwards
high white alto-cumuli proceed steadily west

★

connoisseurs by now
of squall, downpour and drench

          (*you'll be all right atween the showers*
          the boatman said as we disembarked)

weather sweeps in from the west
wind so strong it blows the pelting rain
horizontally over our heads as we hunker
          in the lee of the half-height walls
of the oldest house in northwest Europe

dry and snugly sheltered, squatting on our heels
on a Neolithic farmer's living room floor

*

people friendly, grounded
       always ready for a chat
somewhere where everyone knows everyone

       swadge: to sit back and rest after eating

       'four' pronounced phooerr

Michael's family:
here on the island since the eleventh century

*

The bakery bakes bread on Wednesday and Saturday – you get it hot from the oven. They can't easily send it off the island. It's a matter of sustainability – you don't want to build up your work-force, and then the winter storms are bad enough so there's no boats, and then you lose all the contracts. So they mostly make biscuits and oat-cakes and things with a longer shelf-life – a week of storms with no boats makes no difference to those.

*

curlews, lapwings, snipe, golden plovers and linnets
feed in the fields

grey seals
       with white whiskers
sit up head and shoulders out of the water
watch us with alert and curious eyes

fulmars, gannets and gulls soar above the sea
rise on updrafts, wheel on gusts, or
let their flight be
       slowly bent from its path
by the unabating, incessant westerly

*

in the small
airport
departure lounge

the clock
is wrong

Westray & Papa Westray

Andrew Taylor

Analogue

weekend reading
ink stains
load a
memory bottle

by treading steps
annually
quiet wisdom

of the wild
and general
pace

of walking
through streets
with cast iron
street signs

rusted moulded
letters

birdsong dust
in cobblestone tracks
layered history

Fit the bones reward collars that have been scrubbed clean. Names hidden from view, an appropriate side shift. Like hidden photographs between pages as the words are read aloud, it is the knowing, the travelling and buying of French bread at Sunday markets with the words etched.

★

Long White Split Tin strip then wrap cables prepare for transportation A50 neon spray Diesel engine tick meet at the bakery like we usually do waterfront rendezvous collar turned shoes scuffed blast of river colour amidst courtyard grey bread brown paper wrap a traditional bake

★

Sitting with Alex Katz Pansies and Tulips outside a Ferry is battling the tide it is a Saturday in March in Liverpool and a girl in DM boots stares longingly at *Full Moon 1988* it could have been us at the gallery opening in 1988 when it all began you in Liberty Print me in 501s

★

Train composition poster line up arranged fireworks spark Le Pont don't fall asleep with wet hair skim pebbles Polaroid sidewalk overcoat shelter radios on the blink maybe just one more coffee by the fire before we enter tunnels spot tags track clatter ball bearing can rattle

★

Twelve hours in between a snowdrop walk manufactured pictorial hall footprint mapped rent the cabin for £25 day starts 5.45 a.m. with song arguably ends at 5.45 p.m. a version of the same song analogue treatment at its best set the room for great white spaces & valve silence
i.m. Mark Hollis

Maria Stadnicka

Poetics

I

I had a disagreement with a poetry master
about wolves. And talking made me think
that I, too, had the same great fear
of words living forever, but said nothing.

I watched birds flying at low altitude,
tongue knotted twisting commas
and stops came out of my mouth.

The poet walked away, locked himself
in a room with many doors but no handles.
Outside, his wolf sat on command guarding exits.

Mine wanted to jump from a cloud
straight into the blank page.
A child passed by and said
wolves don't exist on paper. Only in flesh.

II

The soldier, like a poet, awaits
the start of her fight, waving
at people she does not know.
They remind her of home.
Once they all go to sleep,
she measures and trims
the infinite distance between
rooms concealed in her heart.

The poet, like a soldier, does
not have rooms. Her heart bears

its own weight, her story
is smithereens and smoke.
The poet would sleep anywhere
just to be in the same town
with you. She does not have
her own place in the world yet.

Survival Skills

They ask me to eat earth
and kneel on the grass. I bite my tongue
as the soil talks back in our language.

I show them how the tar makes
the best chewing-gum when picked
off the pavement after a heatwave.

Our mirror reflects the sun into the windows
of speeding cars; the drivers' faces light up
like overexposed photographs.

The first to snap a bird's neck
gets a lollipop from Father Michael.
My hands flutter, the wings
knot around my wrist.

I hold my breath. We give it a burial
behind the Laundry Block. One of us
swings Father's censer over the grave.

My fist up to my face whistles
all things bright. Across the garden, a robin
watches the myrrh burning to ashes.

John Phillips

Here

Language you
live in

this silence
because I

need you to
say to

whoever is
listening

nothing
which is said

will be
enough to

make sense
of what will

or will not
happen yet

your failure
is mine

unless
neither of

us end
being treacherous

which is
unlikely.

Shade

If we resemble
meaning,

it's only

the shadow
a light

casts

we are blind
to see.

Refusal

The secret of words is
they don't want to

say anything. Given the
chance each

insists on
silence.

Rimas Uzgiris

I, Myself, am Hell

The spacecraft drifts to its destination.
The illusion of floating on a vast black sea,
rocking, rolling, rock-a-my baby, on… But
reality is swift, and the captain speeds to his target,
watching the screen, like an arrow shot by Zeno –
faster, faster, never to arrive. The cargo in the hold
mews from time to… whenever it ceases to be.
Hell is other people, he thinks, ergo family.
He learned that at school: Sartre, Huis Clos.
He closed the doors on them aeons ago.
The red planet now looms like a dream, grows –
faster, faster, approaching light, the seconds slow,
then die. One red eye, a wide grin, bleeding gums,
sin: the mirror, this morning, looks quite grim.

Burnt Mancusian

The mouse is forced into the maze
As the ball falls into the machine,
Like my eyes as they stray on the streets
And my love as it spills on the sheets.

Some claim we should not speak of beauty.
(Let's see.) It tapers: an old chimney
From the factory floor up to the cloud
That lies over Manchester like a shroud.

Red bricks run down to brown: a Siena
Without a name – Burnt Mancusian
Dilapidation turning lion to dove, former grace
Entombed in forms that are more than a face,

Like your façade as you say good night –
The grace, swiftness, and skylark delight.
While I clatter over figures red and black,
Dazed, a dove in light, before my silent flight.

Early Renaissance

We walked into the store where
The anime had started to storm.
Carlo Crivelli, I said. He's dead,
Replied Thom, try the deli next door.

What door? We wandered the streets
Until Hesperus sank into the sun.
You spied a babe lying on useless tracks
Among nettles, thistles, and bentgrass.

I could hardly hear the speakers announce
That an annunciation had come about,
For a wicked lark was warbling in a larch,
While cars and trucks lurched on and out.

Whose maculate body was fit to outfit whom?
Phosphorus was enough to illuminate our room.

John Seed

Poussin Hegel Eclogue

one knee
on the ground
a shepherd

points at the
letter R
his shadow

seems to point
at his shadow's
head

the origin the
hopeless origins
of art

another
shepherd staring
at the beautiful

woman
points at
too

love was
not in
their eyes

too many
photons
pattering

dry
leaves scrape
on stone

et in arcadia
ego   paradise
a park or

garden shade
reading a tomb's
inscription

moment forms
the moments
form

all our hopes
divided
into rivers

figured
streams in
waves of

silver
currents tide
its fall

from
Maidenhead to
Brentford

twenty feet
every ten miles
but then

to the Nore
sixty miles
seven feet

chill surface
in endless
summer Arcadia

a place away
from the
water's edge

amphitheatre
metropolis
shapes as

it recedes
from
the banks

a second
amphitheatre
rising green

beyond the first
south from
west to east

high grounds of
Richmond Wimbledon
blue-grey shimmer

the Mole Gap
Box Hill Ranmore
eye lost where

light fades in
scribed over
stone moss

green mounds
grown nettles
brambles

calls in
the last
of day

when philosophy
paints its
grey on grey

then
has a form of
life grown old

what we
want always
too late

who you were
promise kept
and not kept

out of
reach the
little green lamp

blinking
across water
on silent wings

the owl of
Minerva takes
flight only as

night falls the
owl of Minerva's
flight

begins into dusk
began

horizon after

horizon into

Miranda Lynn Barnes

Becoming Peregrine

The eyes. Indignant, unblinking. Gold rings
infinitely brighter than November sun.

A still, feathered
weight.

Dipping down, floating above the grass,
the mottled angel of silence comes, quieter

than God.
Today's sky is a clear piercing cry.

A feroxism. What pulls on the leash
as the clouds become magnets.

The sky is grass. What I'm hungry for
is cast through air, then falls,

and as I follow it, wings circling,
unfurling, a fan of brown blades

hurls the world upside down.

The Apple Tree and the Moon

I never heard the apples fall at night. The apple tree held the full, bright moon in its upper branches.

Morning came, with more of those yellow fruits in the grass. Gravity was secretive but far from powerless.

My grandmother is named for a moon. My grandmother's moon orbits the wing of Saturn's rings. My grandmother is named for flowing water. My middle name is a waterfall she gave to me.

My grandma gathers the apples carefully looking for the good ones, and stews them in a pot.

Maybe you don't know: I am also a moon,
one that is small, and orbits her planet closely.

I climbed the lower branches when I was small, until I could climb higher. I climbed but could never reach the moon. I picked an apple that looked perfect, and dropped it to the ground.

When Newton sat in his garden, the apple dropped and rolled to him.

When Newton threw the moon, it tethered round the Earth and grew a stem.

Two hundred miles away from here in Lincolnshire his tree still grows, on its third set of roots, producing rare apples late into the autumn.

I am half the world away.

Tamar Yoseloff

Jade

Fine and smooth and cold
but against the flesh it fires,

old stone, healer for what fails,
death can't pale its lustre,

dredged from the river to make
objects of desire: a likeness

of the Buddha, belly polished
to a shine with many wishes;

or a tomb suit stitched with gold,
sized to fit its wearer, passed away –

until his past returns, dredged up
with grave goods: dagger and idol,

his city idyll, built to skim clouds,
gone to ground, gone for good.

★

In this whorl of green a world,
mineral galaxy, nephrite bright –

her beads, passed down to me,
I warm them against my neck,

my breathing body yanked back
from death – I've never prayed

but in these spheres they say
is heaven, unfathomable ocean;

if nothing more they bind me
to her, flesh of her flesh,

perhaps even in disease, a slow
release in her body, passed down,

down – now she is ash and bone
I take what I must take.

★

The circle serves to fascinate –
we move in and out of world

linked by love, the steady clock
of our hearts. She and I stood

before the emperor's new suit,
his last, guessing its weight, heavy

enough to keep his body under,
while his soul flew to wherever

souls escape. She is no place now,
but her things occupy my space:

this jade, colour of what you see
when you look deep in water,

like reaching through the sky
to hold a little piece of earth.

Mark Goodwin

Snow Thick on Beinn Sgritheall Down to Around 600m, Very Early Spring, 2018

Beinn Sgritheall's ab
rupt snow-g

host   (a season's
       spook soon

up-ground riding   to
        melt)

     above

brown/green mot
tle-slopes & bir ch
-t

  will

     above

hamlet arn Is dale's
hist orical intri cacies its wisps of

  lived   appearing to

day as   day's
solid de tailed

house-shapes st rung a

      long loch

        shore while

Sleat's Sound and
Loch Hourn's

h a r d f l o w l a p s

•

all

as all
ways

from sky

to snow's   sc   r   oll

down

to

ground

sounded

Note: Beinn Sgritheall (pronounced *ben skree-huhl*) rises above the hamlet of
Arnisdale & the north shore of Loch Hourn. *Sgritheall* is Gaelic for *a scroll*.

Wet Rhyolite

for Chris Jones, and his patience

Glyder Fach's mist
-greased blocks &

                    hard

splinters of distance
scattered to craze to

                be got
                    across

each   step   a
    slip

                pery puzzle as

spikes & crenulations
ghoul through fog the

                    whole

ankle-cracking-and
-shin-ski

        nning lot

                    hard

                            as a poem a

    bout to be

                                    done just

so but

no

t

ju

st

ye

t

Robert Sheppard

from Bad Idea: overdubs of Michael Drayton's *Idea*

To the Reader of these Sonnets

I hear one shriek, 'He's no formal poet!
He can't write, rolling his pastry-prose through
white space into shapelets… Just look at it!'
You are too quick to judge, my english rose.
I hang out inside these sonnets, punching
echoes into new shape, because I take
poetry as the investigation
of complexity through the means of form.
You shallow censor, you'll hate these ones too.
From the depths of national despair, I roar,
gallows humour. I uncouple each 'I-
dea', bash my brains until opinion bleeds,
interrupt the passionate civilities
of Drayton's lines, until dying laughs.

(Overdub of Sonnet XXIV)

XI

You're not alone when you take out a loan
or when you transpose my self into your being:
you a Brexit monad, me a digital nomad
whose algorithm predicts a rupture in common-
sense that threatens to translate subjectivation.
For the worse, maybe. But in this swap-shop love
we'll be absent to ourselves, lost in furtive spurts,
subject to visa checks at the Chequers border:
the uniform blue passport, the fixed biometrics.
What was mine alone sings in you as I bristle

with the collective: level applause for Corbyn's pitch.
You say: I rather like that Jacob Rees-Mogg.
          Disenchantment! I want my bits back.
          I'll loan out my own lyric intersubjectivity.

27th September 2018

XIII

In these lines your words are scribbled over
but we can still see your Idea through the rust.
That scratched diamond is still worth pawning,
and your stained slips still Calvin Klein declare!
I'm drawing dirty pictures of your letters,
every bodily fluid ink, every body a script.
Under-read but written over,
every sign is your unfinished sigh.
Every body casts its shadow: spectral optics
slips one under every step she takes
dancing to the podium on conference speech day,
gluing her to every bad promise.
          May's Shadow wrong-foots her once more:
          some think it's Corbyn, but we know worse.

11th October 2018

XVI (An Allusion to the Phœnix)

You're bored by his allusion: a bird in fake flames
flaps in false equivalence,
like the Brexit 50p minting cut-price independence.
Your beauty must be clattering down his exchange
rates too. He negotiates with your Self, your sacred pyre,
causing a stink about your sovereign right
to burn up EU free movers. By the time

he gets to Phœnix you'll be rising, the latest star
to star in his starry story, to outshine and burn
forever! You kindle pyromantic futures:
Let's increase consumption as freedom nears;
they won't notice we're feeding them charcoal.
> A burnt-out Citroën on an M20 sliproad,
> his poem will leave you no-deal.

1st November 2018 XIX

XIX

You cannot simply say leave. No deal! Know why?
There was a time once for give and take;
but now the research group with no research papers,
the bile of those who hop from hot to cold, stays.
Will you remain then? No! Not another plebiscite,
cracking its tattooed knuckles over representation.
No leave, no remain. What then is your question?
Love or hate? Try framing that on a ballot.
Impossible! all say. What next? Paradox as paradigm?
Yes and no, the eternal tautology? Yes:
a hovercraft rules the waves it barely fringes. No,
we're deceived by others', and our own, drifting certainties.
> 'Love and remain …' I think I've got you: then you say,
> 'This year's word is toxic,' and you've lost me.

22nd November 2018

Alasdair Paterson

My life *au contraire*

To trudge head down onwards ever onwards or sink down on the memorial bench with the celebrated view just as darkness falls.

To be observably balding or detectably bewigged. To be mutton dressed as lamb or mutton dressed as *mouton*. To bridle at the term 'curmudgeon' or bite its hand off.

To be innocuous to the blurry point of invisibility or sashay out as a ready-made pin-sharp figure of fun. To buy cartons of the soups you actually prefer or those you can actually open. To take the bait or bite the lip.

To obsess about the Queen's English going to the dogs or smile to think how many years it is since one was favoured with a glimpse of, like, yer actual royal corgi, ken whit ahm sayin pal. To cosy up in bed imagining wage slave ex-colleagues trudging workwards through the rain or get up anyway because standards must be maintained. To refuse the can of worms or rejoice that it does exactly what it says on the tin.

To respect the right to remain silent or show it the instruments of torture. To pimp the engine of slow draggy days or stamp stamp stamp fruitlessly on the brakes. To grieve over your shrinking stock of bosom buddies or rejoice that your imaginary friend is back after all these years.

To take pleasure in family photo albums or be grateful that, for your most vivid memories, no negatives exist. To tell a lie and disappoint an angel or tell the truth and spoil the joke. To make up your mind not to die wondering or sort of feel it's wondering gets you through the day.

To ply charity shops with all the seminal works you'll have no time to read again or find comfort in calculating how many decades it should take to get through all the unread books from the same shops now piled high on the stairs. To get into e-books because therein lies the future or remain convinced that the contours of your personality are best mapped by the titles and editions and colours and inscriptions and marginalia and stains and gaps and general wear and tear on your shelves. To favour the future tense because it works or because it will only work for a while.

To drop everything and just go – or check all the switches first and wonder about making sandwiches. To pride yourself on the crispness of your memories or on the clarity of your conviction that whatever you remember isn't likely to have been that way at all. To remain a fan of the words "happily ever after" or concede that they are comprehensively undermined by the words "funeral plan".

To maintain as an article of faith that the stairs must have a top and a bottom or voice your suspicion that the prison might be infinite. To be moved by the spiritual import of the central panel of the triptych or more impressed by the colour harmonies and the rendering of the drapery. To feel a glow at how awfully nice it's going to be among the saved souls in the left-hand panel or allow the thought to cross your mind that after-life in the right-hand panel looks, by comparison, pretty damn lively.

To encounter in the mirror the furrowed lineaments of accumulated wisdom or the air coming out of an old balloon. To be satisfied that all those regrettable compromises were necessarily part of the strategy to change the system from within, or just a little guilty that the smokescreen of system change allowed you to enjoy all the fruits of these compromises. To buy into the notion that human evolution is driving us into a world of new possibilities or, on empirical evidence, beyond the viability of our teeth.

To be borne away on the currents of Renaissance polyphony or feel increasingly unembarrassed that the soundtrack of your life was, is and ever shall be cheap music. To dismay the family with ill-considered proposals for the comeback tour or inappropriate quips about guid tunes played on auld fiddles. To tease the children with plans to spend their inheritance or get on with spending it and let them find out later.

To feel the need to cling to the guard-rail or the urge to set foot on the space beyond just because. To stare into glass after filled glass hoping your face will eventually surface or slowly submerge. To reach out and touch life with your old confidence or be embarrassed by how cold your hands are these days.

To try again and fail again or think it may be easier all round to establish a more generous definition of success. To conclude that what doesn't kill you makes you stronger or, on reflection, stranger. To watch sleeplessly as night turns into day, as a condemned man waits hoping at least that the last breakfast will be up to scratch, or come to groggily in a susurration of dispersing dreams like a castaway washed up in the surf.

To deduce that it was Colonel Mustard in the conservatory with the candlestick or your parents in the lounge with the White Heather Club. To go out to the bluebell wood for a stocktake of your life or decide that one life is not long enough to account for this rock, this rivulet, these flowers, this dance of leaves. To lie under a hedge pondering whether to make your indelible contribution to regional poetry with 'The man with the blue tractor' or with '13 ways of eating a blackbird'.

To experience an epiphany of sorts re the title of the final volume of your autobiography: 'Over the hill: or at least somewhere thereabouts I seem to remember, but I could be wrong, hmm'. To climb into bed exhilarated by a good day getting your long-nourished book project underway or admit as darkness falls that the title really says it all. To face the fact that your style all along has been grappa with a dash of curaçao or Kurosawa with a dash of Capra.

To deplore the cruelties of the Roman arena or dream a little dream about which of your contemporaries you might send out across the bloody sand like Orpheus, armed only with a harp, to charm the wild beasts. To back the proposition that about suffering they were never wrong, the old masters, or wonder whether being eaten and excreted by something beaky throughout eternity can really still be part of the Church's teaching. To congratulate yourself that, like an oyster, you produced the pearl that is your family, or have an inkling that your family is more inclined to see you as the piece of grit.

To despair when your favourite pétanque shot, the high lob with side-spin, puts your back out, or feel a certain smugness at having incurred a sports-related injury. To look forward to another twenty years behind the wheel or acknowledge that if you were your passenger you'd be fidgeting with that door-handle too. To be convinced that your investigations are bringing you closer to an understanding of the universe and your place in it, or to an acceptance that your life and the universe have been, in their varying degrees, a great waste of time.

To support with pride the myriad developments and improvements transforming your home city or feel wistful that the silhouette of its skyline and the graph of your brainwaves are becoming quite divergent. To say that nothing can come out of nothing or decide to say nothing. To bob around happily in the amniotic fluid of nostalgia broadcasting or suffer nightmares in which the celebrity undead of yesteryear crawl jerkily out of the TV set.

To like nothing better than to linger by the window in the last hour of the day – or close the curtains uneasily, reflecting that, where an estate is haunted, a window is just another turn of the screw. To go out to the hazel wood because a fire is in your head or on a quest for evidence that the Ordnance Survey has been infiltrated by psychogeographers. To be in two minds as to whether you might have been happier as a free man in Paris or a fireman on Harris.

To view the veteran maverick politician with an increasing weariness or continue to give him the benefit of the doubt, especially since you're so often mistaken for him in public these days. To take after your father in his ability to make a garden or your grandfather in his ability to make a garden and move house. To launch another search-and-destroy mission among the flower beds or finally appreciate that nothing there is as compelling as the languorous depredations of snails.

To give away all your material possessions and move to a mountain hut for indefinite moon-viewing and composition of short verses, wine glass in hand, or calculate in mid-clearance that among the bric-a-brac you've been accumulating for sixty years there must surely be some items worth a good wee bit in the collectables market. To decide that your next and maybe last work will be called 'Closing oppositions or 70 dilemmas to resolve before you die'. To discover on a recount that it will have to be called 'Closing oppositions or 62 dilemmas to resolve before you die'.

To trudge head down onwards ever onwards or, you know what, just stop here.

Greta Ambrazaitė

translated by Rimas Uzgiris

liturgical

I.

I remember how I fell
on the kitchen floor
and cried like a child
as if in the middle of the store
twenty years ago
while you were warming your wine,
dripping tears, I slaughtered
half a flock
of God's lambs,
I really missed the silence

II.

the butcher shop girl
was far too pretty,
let me know if you need any help,
as she cleaned the clots of red wine

III.

in truth, I am a little wolf
in white, outgrown clothing

IV.

the sun was shining too brightly that day:
don't be angry, but most days
are beyond my recall

V.

we stop by in the evening
at five o'clock, after mass
because wine
was thirty percent off:
I'm a child who remembers
a drunk father and the cutting
midwinter sun

VI.

I've been warming the same wine
for twenty years now,
I think
I've earned
this longing

openness

in the corner of the refectory,
there, where soup is poured for others,
a doctor of mathematics,
wearing plaid pajamas,
approaches a blossoming flower,
his chosen, incarnadine wife,
and recites numbers to her:
5, 30, 68, 91,
only then do I understand where I am,
and what this place is called

carefully drawing a mandala,
the kindergarten teacher
whispers in a barely comprehensible voice
that all the music has been taken from her,
and with her earphones wrapped in sheets,
she says, it's a bad connection here

the roadway engineer is always enquiring,
and asks me to lunch every day,
for example, in the middle of the ocean

loved ones, holding hands,
walk past me as if on stage,
above their sewn up lips
ring little bells of wind

mysticism is made for people
who haven't found their place in life,
said Jean-Paul Sartre

common experience here is just
a wild, rotten tree
that needs to be pruned

on the other side of the river

we threw bread crumbs from the bank,
somewhere not unlike the old Left Bank,
and it was good, even though I knew
we weren't feeding ducks here, but rats

Toon Tellegen

translated by Judith Wilkinson

Francis of Assisi

I saw Francis of Assisi run
                along the borders of hysteria,
chased by dogs and wolves and tsars with their boyars
                and jaundice, scarlet fever, diphtheria

the sun went down and I a saw a field mouse
                trying to slip away quietly
through the grass at my feet

I was alone,
I had to choose between the known and the unknown

it was November
and the rain began to beat down violently
and someone called out:
'hey, you, lagging behind, get a move on,
or you'll die, cold and empty-handed!'

Charon

In his freshly tarred house full of young cobwebs,
on the banks of his green river,
while swallows skimmed past the last willows
and loose coins shimmered in the grass,
he lay sleeping.
His boat had sprung a leak or it was too late
or the wind was too strong or he was tired.
I wasn't planning to embark myself,
but I wanted to know who he was,

as a precaution,
and perhaps hear the lapping of the waves
and the sighs coming from the other side.
It was the middle of a day and when he woke up
and saw me standing at his window,
he immediately began to comment on my nails,
which he couldn't see,
and my croaky voice,
which he couldn't hear,
and my thoughts,
which he couldn't read, or perhaps he could,
and my shabby raincoat. What about yours, I replied,
pointing at all its holes.
I walked away, without knowing where to, he called after me.
And when I looked back, tired of being so hesitant,
he was taking someone else with him. She was standing upright,
alone, in the middle of his boat.
She was wearing a green rose between her green-painted lips
and waved
from the middle of the river,
or was she coming towards me?
I saw wisps of smoke, reed and blurry figures
and a glistening other shore
and I no longer knew
if I was still there
or here already.

A Fairy-Tale

The emperor took off his coat
and all the people took off their coats.

The emperor hesitated
and all the people hesitated wholeheartedly.

The emperor put his coat back on
and they all hastily put their coats back on, fumbling,
wrestling with sleeves, stumbling.

The emperor was cold
and everyone shivered, stamped their feet, froze, fell
to their deaths

and a boy said,
a boy in a red coat holding his dead father's hand:
'You were going to show me the truth.
Where is the truth?'

Only Just

I live happily ever after, but only just,
and there are people who only just love each other forever –

under a tree stands Newton,
gazing at an apple
that only just doesn't fall –
it's evening, it's raining, bedraggled herons are standing stock-still
at the side of a ditch,
while he gazes up passionately –

everything that is impossible is still just possible,
peace only just floats across the infinite countryside.

Notes on Contributors

Clark Allison was born in Glasgow in 1961, although he spent nine years in the 1980s living in Los Angeles. Author of *Temporal Shift/Daubs* (Trombone Press, 1998) and of several poems and reviews appearing in *Notus* and *Stride*.

Greta Ambrazaitė is a Lithuanian poet. Her first book, published in 2018, won the Young Yotvingian Prize, and was named poetry book of the year at the Vilnius Book Fair.

Annemarie Austin lives in Somerset. Her first collection, *The Weather Coming* appeared in 1987. *Very: New & Selected Poems* (Bloodaxe Books, 2008) included work from all of her previous collections, including *On the Border* (1993), *The Flaying of Marsyas* (1995), *Door upon Door* (1999) and *Back from the Moon* (2003). She has since published another collection, *Track* (2014).

Benjamin Balint is a writer and translator living in Jerusalem. His trans-lation of Hagit Grossman's poetry was published by Shearsman Books (*Trembling in the City*, 2016) and other translations have appeared in *The New Yorker*, *Poetry International* and *Crazyhorse*. He is most recently the author of *Kafka's Last Trial* (Picador, 2019). The content of the poems in this issue was occasioned by research for his book *Jerusalem: City of the Book* (co-authored with Merav Mack, Yale University Press, 2019).

Miranda Lynn Barnes is a poet from the US, now resident in the Bristol. Her poems appear or are forthcoming in *New Welsh Reader, Tears in the Fence, Under the Radar, The Compass, The Interpreter's House* and *Lighthouse Journal*. She taught Poetry and other genres for five years at Bath Spa University, where she completed her PhD in Creative Writing in 2017, and where she now serves as Research Publications Librarian.

Alison Brackenbury has a number of collections from Carcanet, most recently a Selected Poems titled *Gallop* (2019). She lives in Cheltenham.

Rachael Clyne is a psychotherapist based in Glastonbury. Her chapbook, *Girl Golem*, was published by 4word in 2018.

Andrew Duncan is a British poet, translator and critic, the majority of whose work is now published by Shearsman Books. Most recent volumes: *On the Margins of Great Empires: Selected Poems* and *Fulfilling the Silent Rules — Inside & Outside in Modern British Poetry 1960-1997* (both 2018). His trans-lation of the poetry of Thomas Kling, *zerodrifter*, is scheduled to appear from Shearsman at about the same time as this issue is released.

Chris Emery was until recently a director of Salt Publishing. He has pub-lished three collections of poetry: *Dr. Mephisto, Radio Nostalgia* and *The*

Departure. He lives in Cromer, Norfolk, with his wife and children.

GERRIE FELLOWS published her most recent collection, *Uncommon Places,* with Shearsman in 2019. A New Zealander by origin, she lives in Glasgow.

ADAM FLINT lives in Berlin. His poetry has been published previously by *Critical Documents, Stand*, and *Blackbox Manifold*, among others.

MARK GOODWIN has several collections from Shearsman, most recently the book *House at Out*, and the chapbook *All Space Away*. Also recently published is *Rock as Gloss* from Longbarrow Press, Sheffield.

LUCY HAMILTON is co-editor of *Long Poem Magazine* and has two collections from Shearsman: *Stalker* (2012, shortlisted for the Forward Prize for best first collection) and *Of Heads & Hearts* (2018).

JERI ONITSKANSKY is an American-born Jungian analyst and poet, based in London for the last 22 years. Her poems have appeared in a number of publications including *Ambit, Magma, PN Review, The Rialto* and *Poetry Review*. Her pamphlet *Call them Juneberries* was an IOTA shot winner and was published by Templar Poetry in 2015.

ALASDAIR PATERSON lives in Exeter. He has two collections from Shearsman: *On the Governing of Empires* and *Elsewhere or Thereabouts*.

JOHN PHILLIPS' most recent book, *Shape of Faith* (2017), is from Shearsman and he has several others, from both British and American publishers. He now lives in Slovenia.

PAUL ROSSITER was born in Cornwall in 1947, and moved permanently to Japan in 1981. He retired from teaching English and applied linguistics at the University of Tokyo in 2012 and in the following year founded Isobar Press. In addition to his four Isobar books, three earlier volumes of his poetry have been published in Japan: *In Daylight* (Printed Matter, 1995), *Monumenta Nipponica* (Saru, 1995), and *The Painting Stick* (Pine Wave, 2005).

ALEXANDRA SASHE has two collections with Shearsman, most recently *Convalescence Dance* (2018). Russian by origin, she lives in Vienna.

KATE SCHMITT's poems have appeared in the *Annual of Urdu Studies, Solstice MFA Anthology*, and *Shearsman*. She lives and works in Central Vermont.

JOHN SEED has published several volumes with Shearsman, including a *New and Collected Poems* (2005), *Smoke Rising* (2015) and *melancholy occurrences* (2018). He lives in London.

ROBERT SHEPPARD has a number of books from Shearsman including *History or Sleep – Selected Poems* (2015) and the curated volume, *Twitters for a Lark: Poetry of the European Union of Imaginary Authors* (2017). 2019 has also seen the publication by Shearsman of a large volume of essays devoted to his work, *The Robert Sheppard Companion*, edited by James Byrne & Christopher Madden.

MARIA STADNICKA is a writer and journalist based in Gloucestershire. Her publications include *Short Story about War* (Yew Tree Press, 2014), *Imperfect* (Yew Tree Press, 2017), *Somnia* (The Knives, Forks and Spoons Press, 2019), *Uranium Bullets* (Červená Barva Press, 2019).

ANDREW TAYLOR's two collections of poetry, *Radio Mast Horizon* (2013) and *March* (2017) are published by Shearsman Books. Recent pamphlets include *Aire* (Red Ceilings Press), *The 140s* (Leafe Press) and *Air Vault* (Oystercatcher Press). He lives and works in Nottingham

TOON TELLEGEN (b. 1941) is a Dutch poet, children's author, and physician. The poems here come from a selected edition of Tellegen's work being published this year by Shoestring Press. Previous publications include *Raptors* (Carcanet Press, 2011) and *A Man and an Angel* (Shoestring, 2013).

JAMES TURNER lives in Exeter. The poems in this issue are part of a series detailing the author's breakdown in 2015, and his battle with depression. He is now feeling better than ever before. He has published two collections: *Forgeries* (Original Plus, 2002) and *A Chance of Love: Sonnets of Two Decades* (Oversteps Books, 2015). He is a regular reader and performer and was Exeter Slam Champion in 2015.

RIMAS UZGIRIS is a poet, translator, editor and critic. His first collection of poems, *North of Paradise*, has recently appeared from Kelsay Books, Utah. He is translator of books by Ilzė Butkutė, Gintaras Grajauskas, Marius Burokas, Aušra Kaziliūnaitė, and Judita Vaičiūnaitė (the last from Shearsman). Uzgiris has contributed significantly as editor and translator to two anthologies: *How the Earth Carries Us: New Lithuanian Poets* and *New Baltic Poets* (Parthian). Recipient of a Fulbright Scholar Grant, an NEA Literature Translation Fellowship, and the Poetry Spring 2016 Award for translations of Lithuanian poetry into other languages, he teaches translation at Vilnius University.

RUSHIKA WICK is a physician and poet with an interest in the human embodiment of social contracts and relationships. She is a student at the Poetry School London and has had work published in various anthologies and magazines including *Ambit* and *Litro* and forthcoming in the *Mechanics' Institute Review* 16, *Flock* and *3:AM* amongst others. She performs poetry regularly including with the *Cold Lips* magazine collective in London and Rough Night Press in Amsterdam.

JUDITH WILKINSON lives in the Netherlands and is both a poet and a translator from Dutch. Shearsman will soon publish her translations of Menno Wigman. She has won many awards, including the Popescu Prize for European Poetry in Translation in 2011, and the Brockway Prize in 2013.

TAMAR YOSELOFF has published five collections, most recently *A Formula for Night: New and Selected Poems* (Seren, 2015). A new collection, *The Black Place*, is due shortly from the same publisher.